Faces of Fantasy
greyscale coloring book

by

Tabz Jones

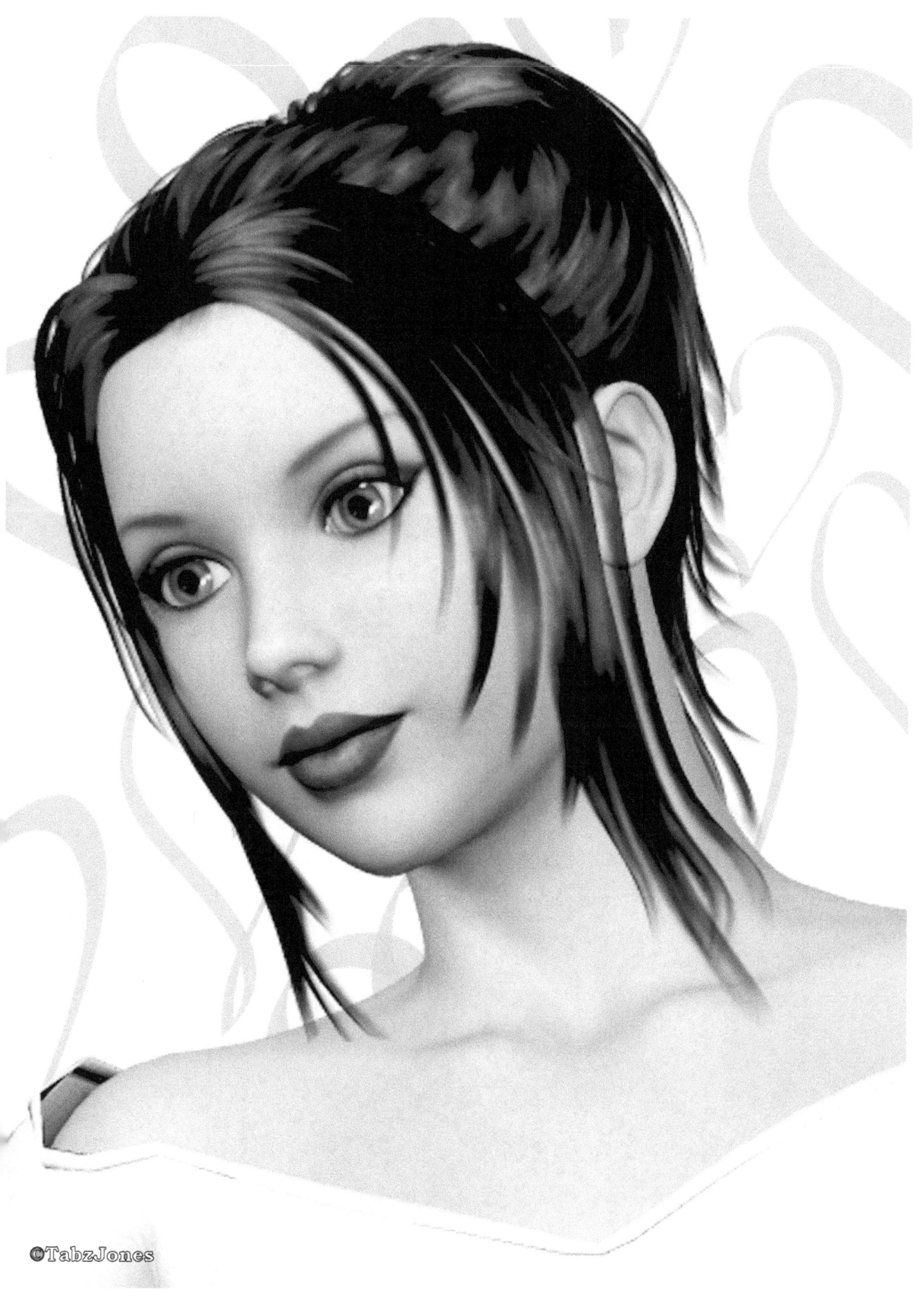

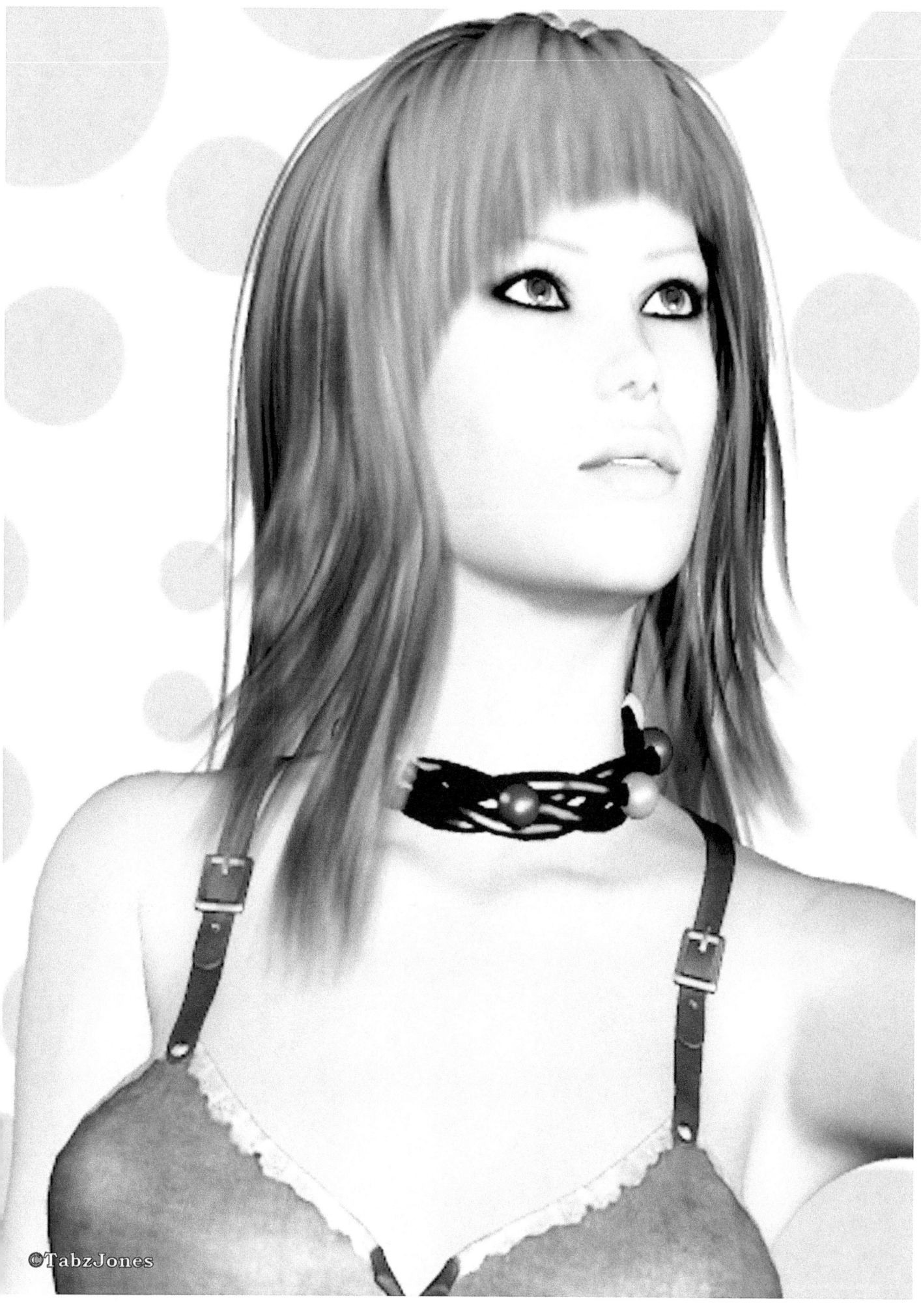

©TabzJones

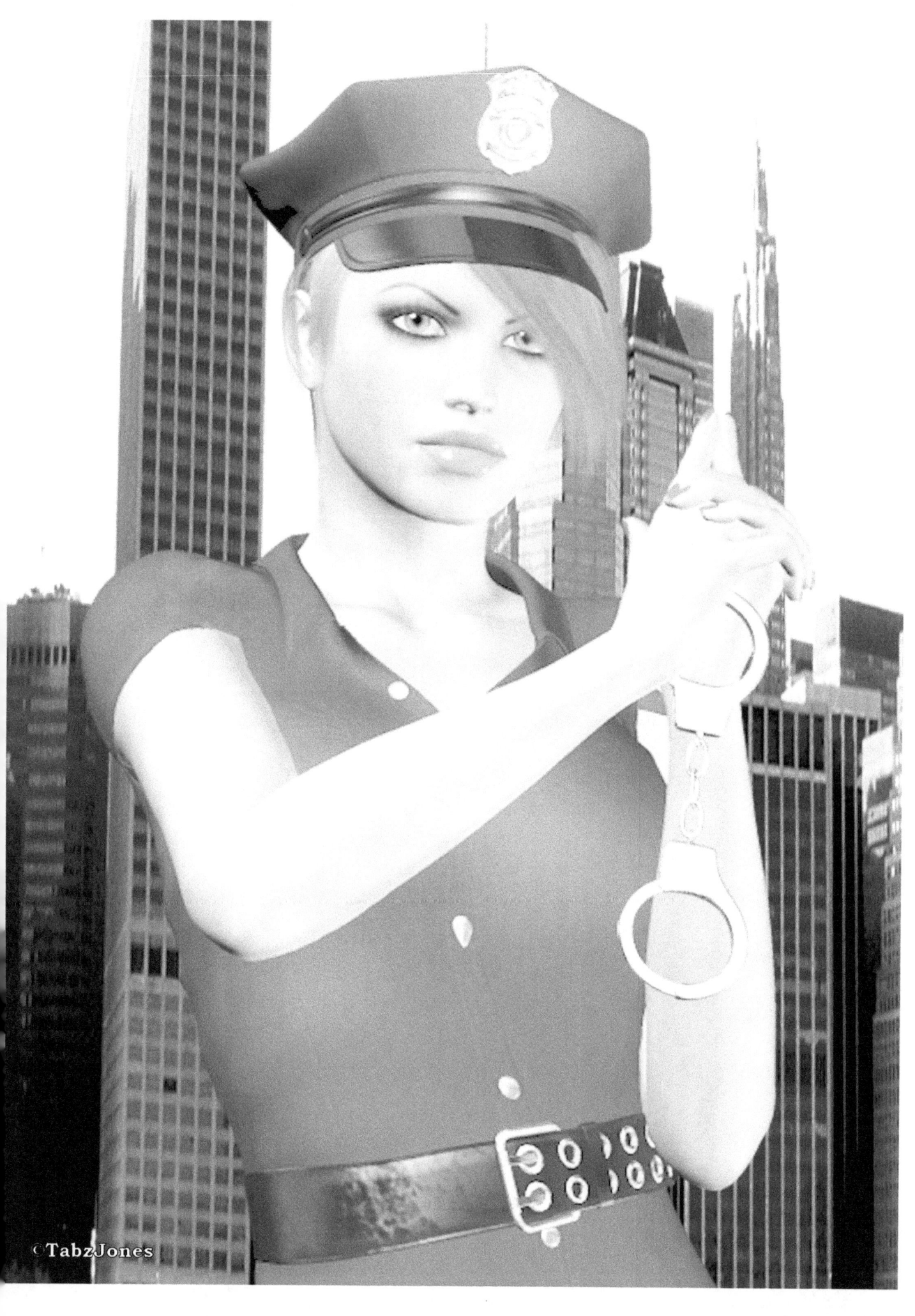

©TabzJones

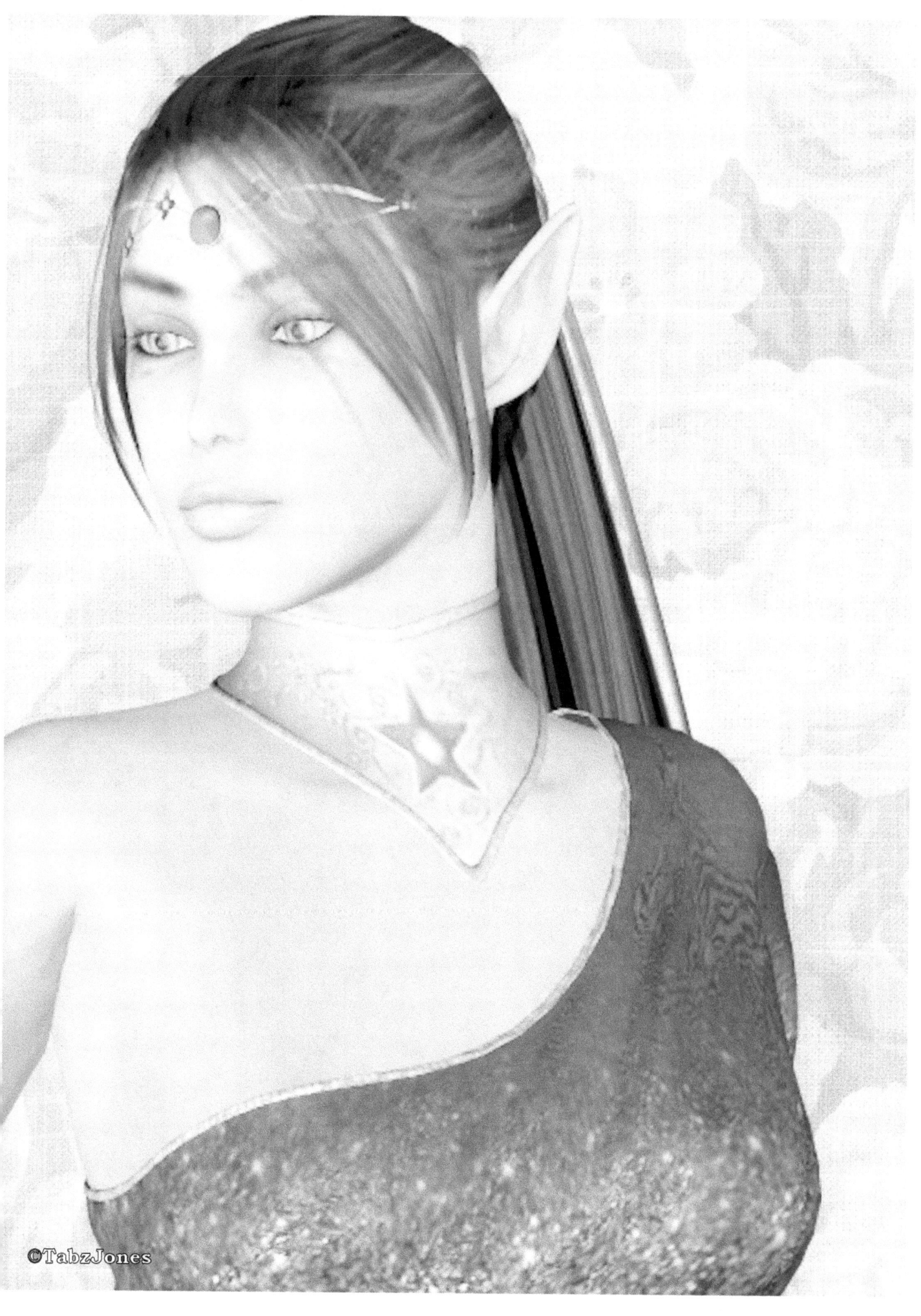

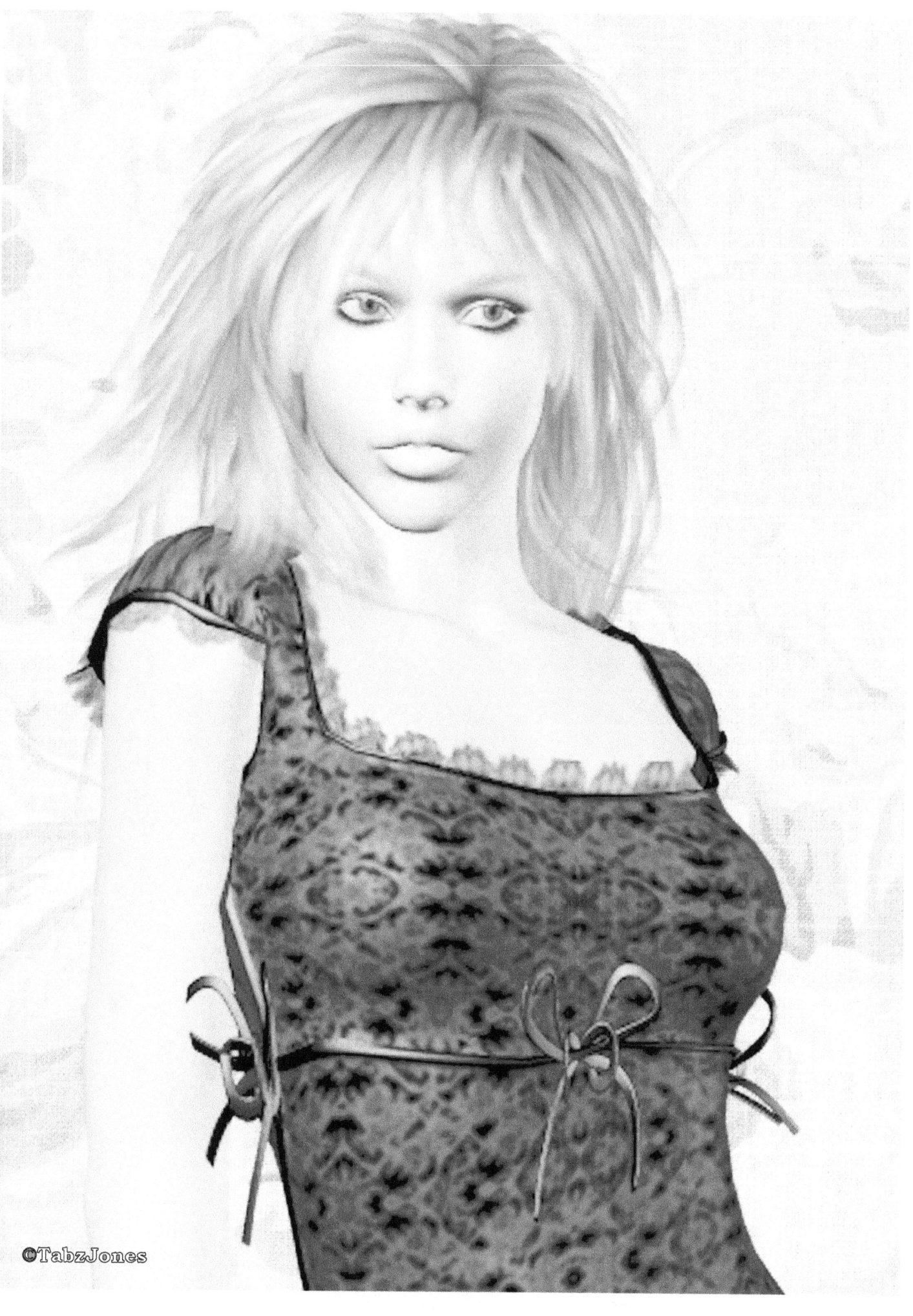

©TabzJones

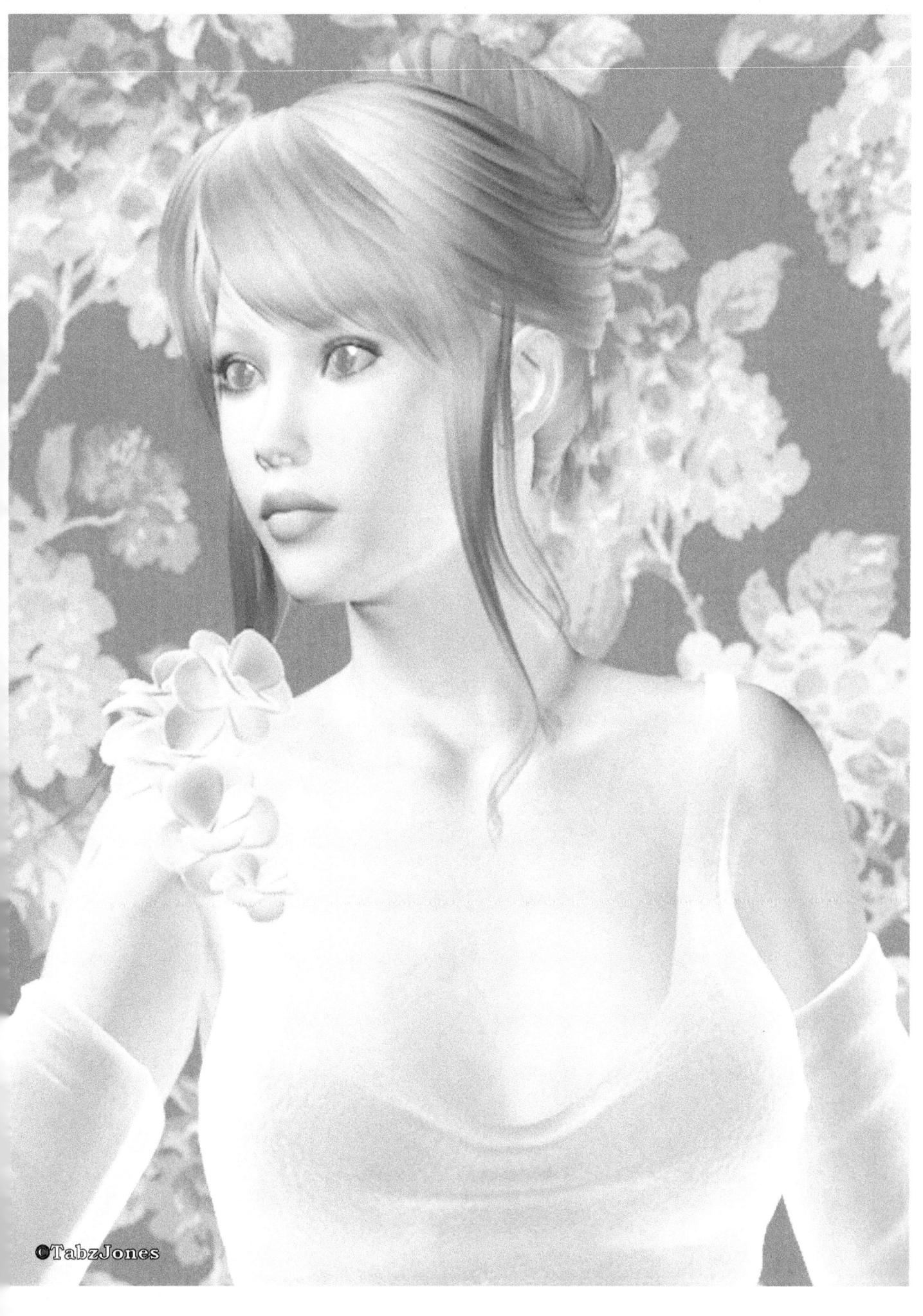

©TabzJones

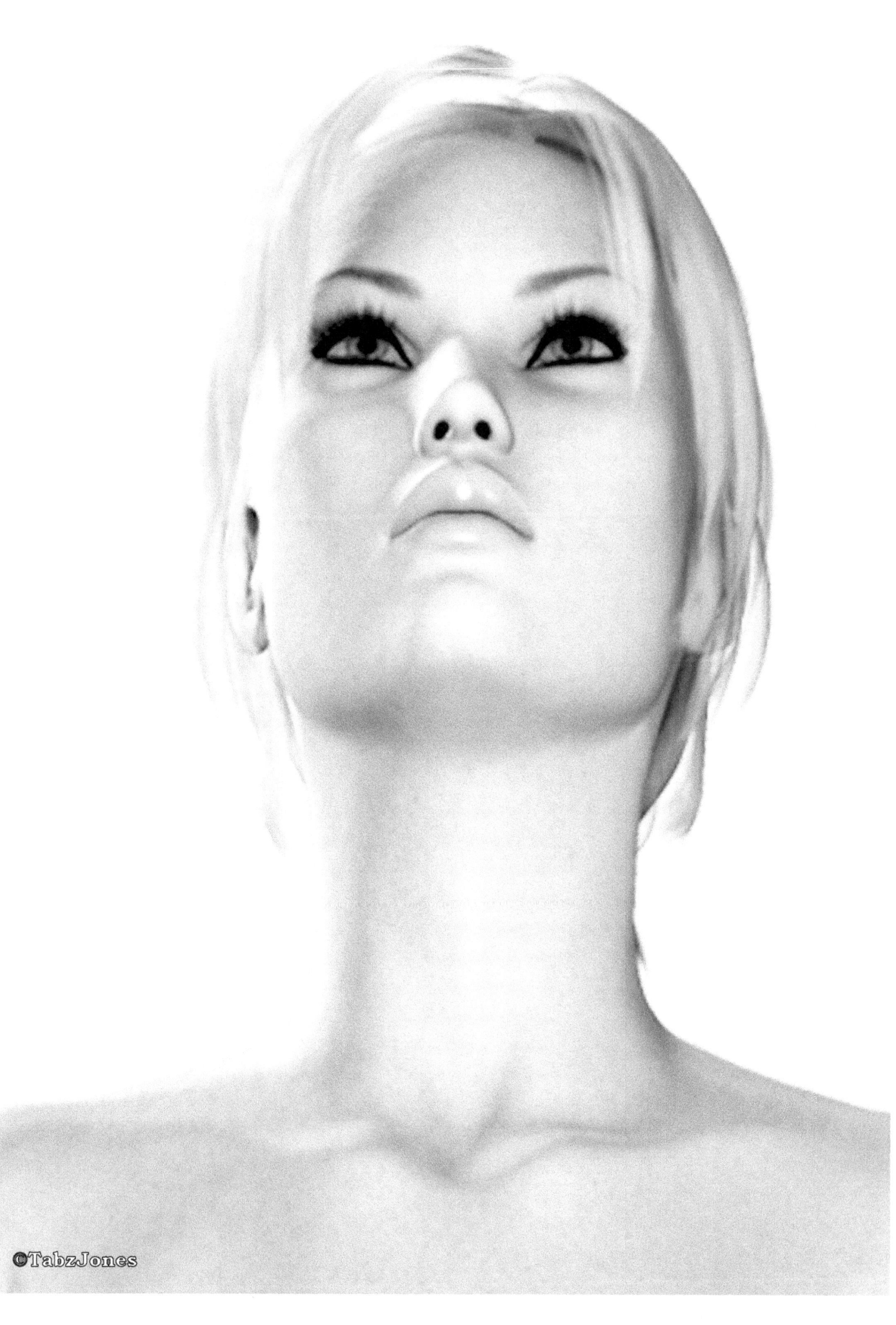

©TabzJones

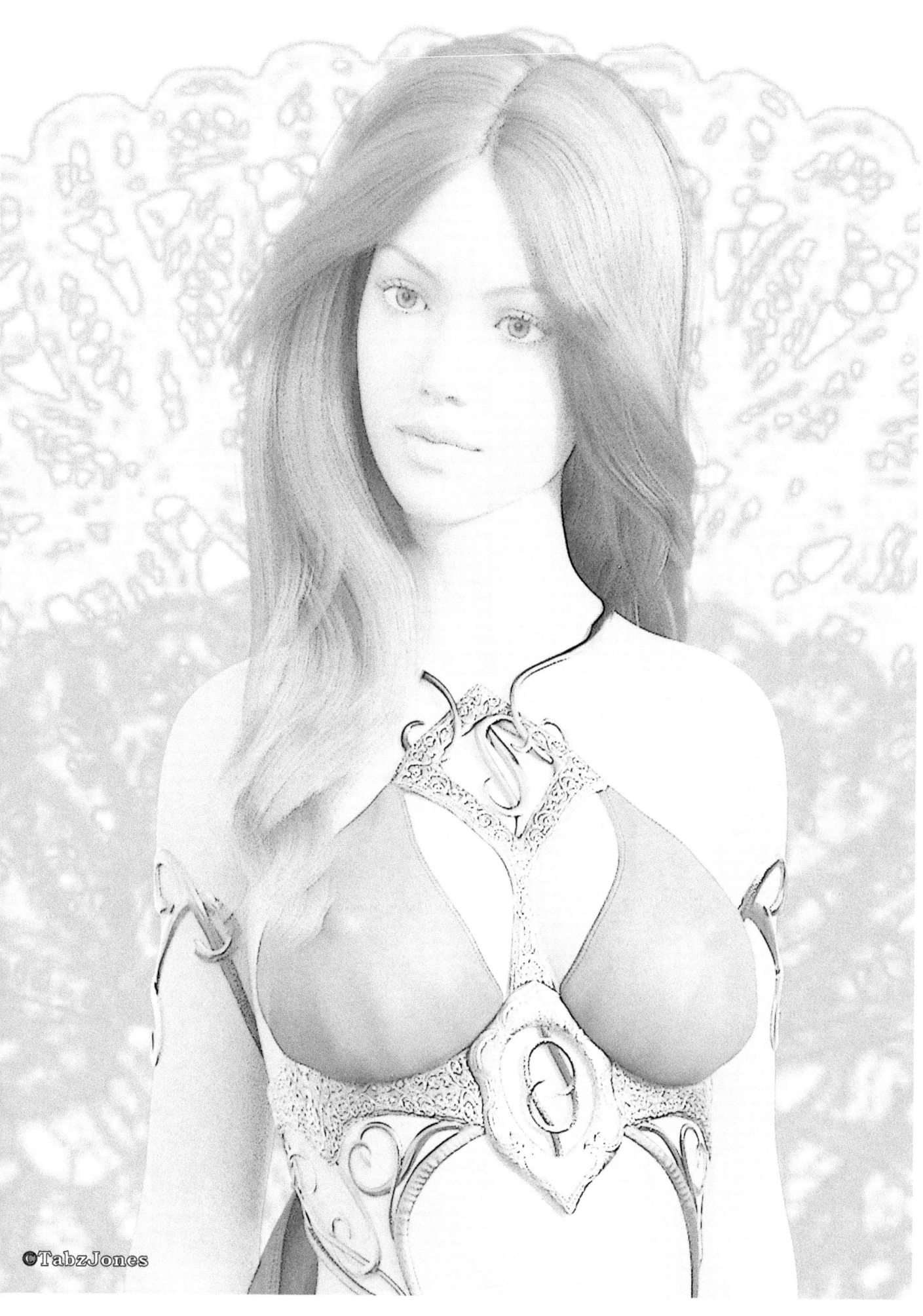

©TabzJones

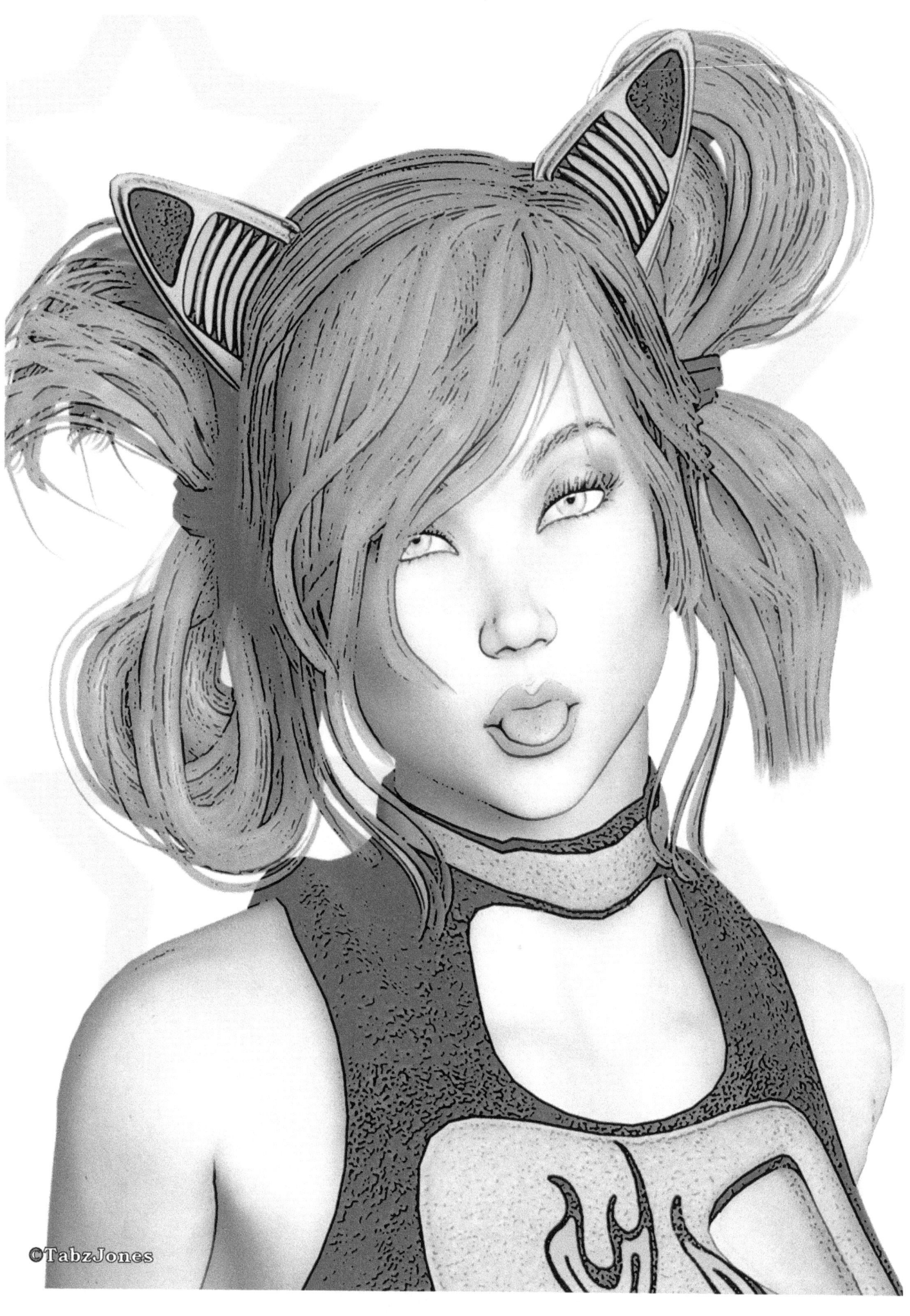

©TabzJones

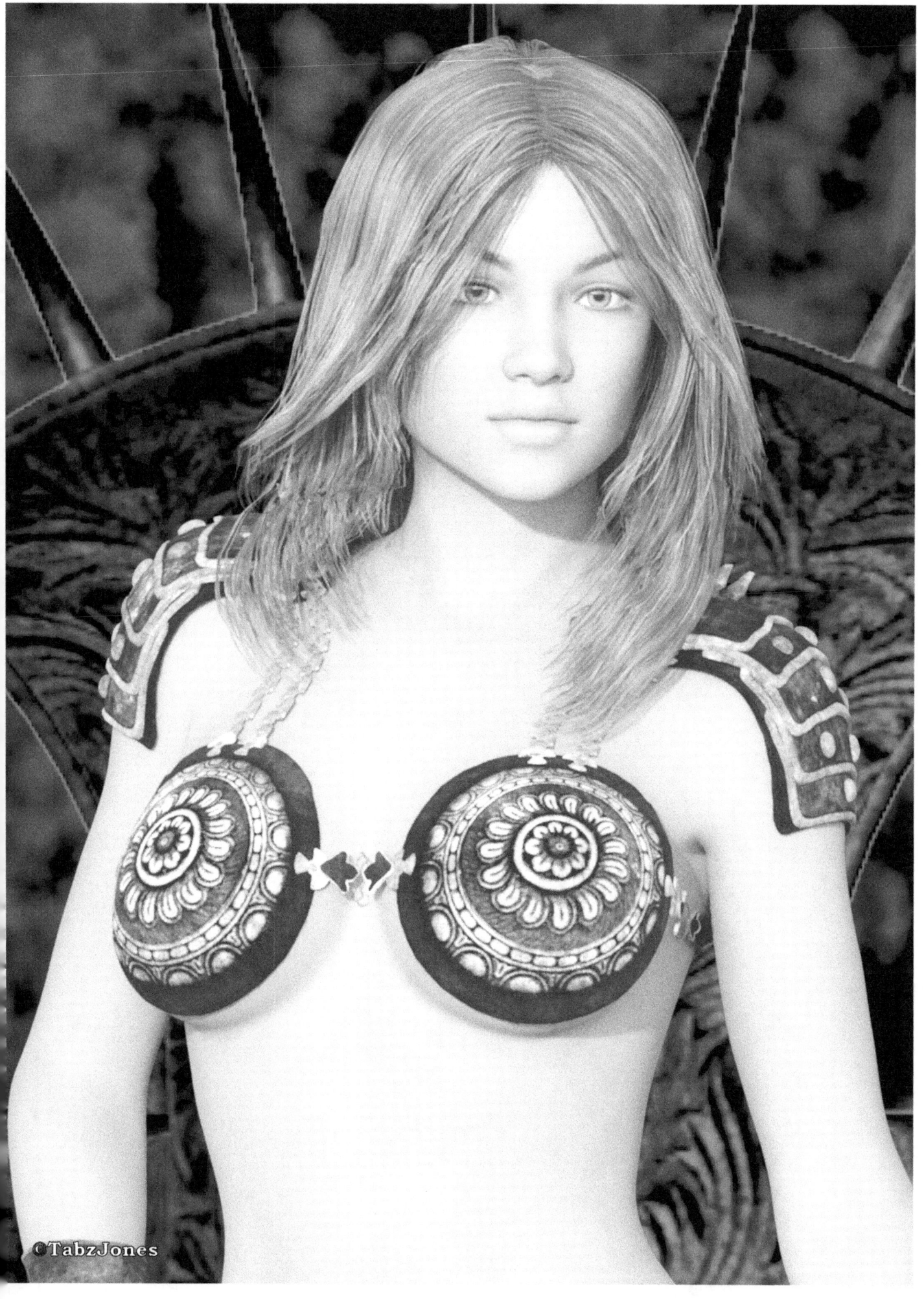
©TabzJones

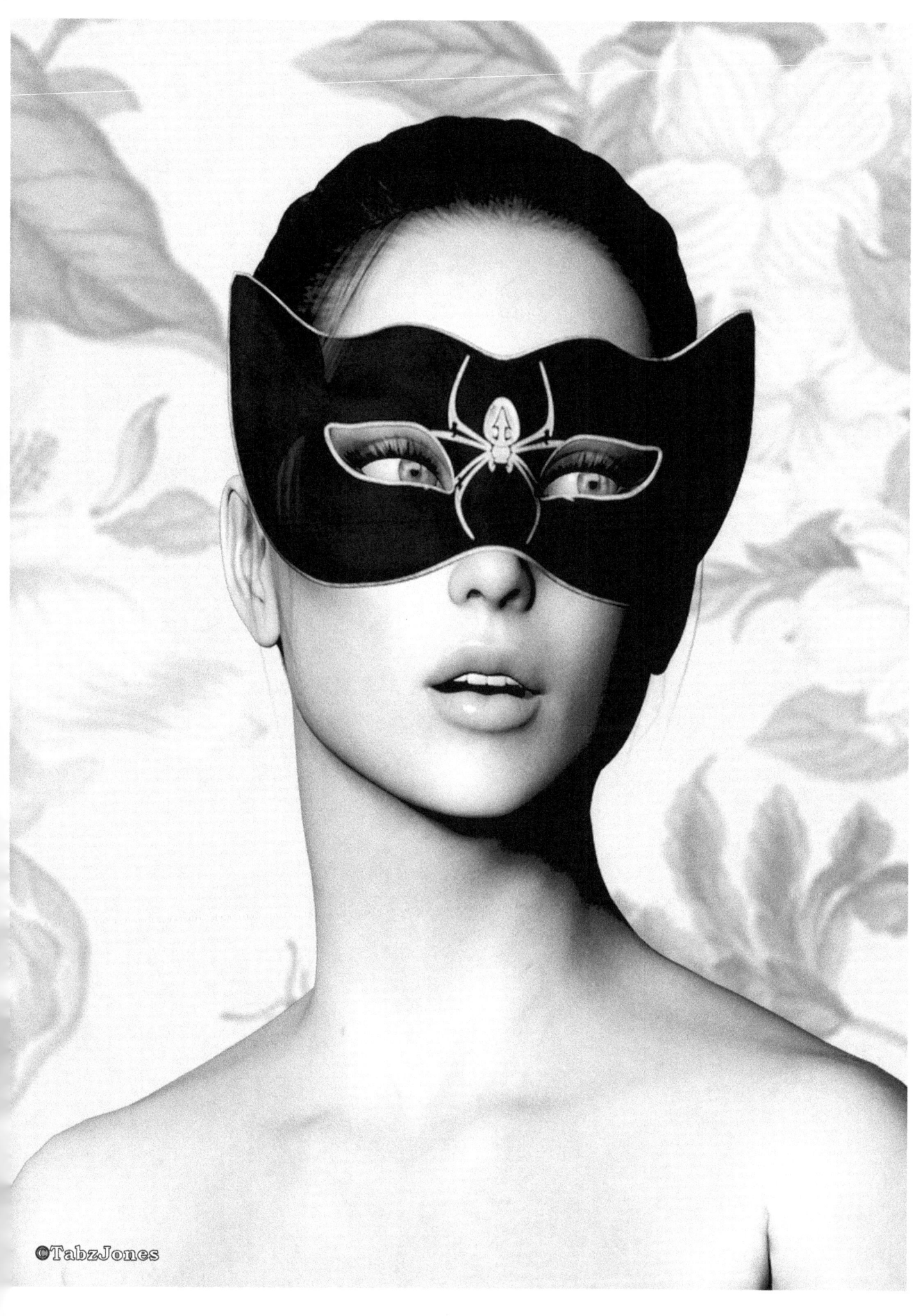

©TabzJones

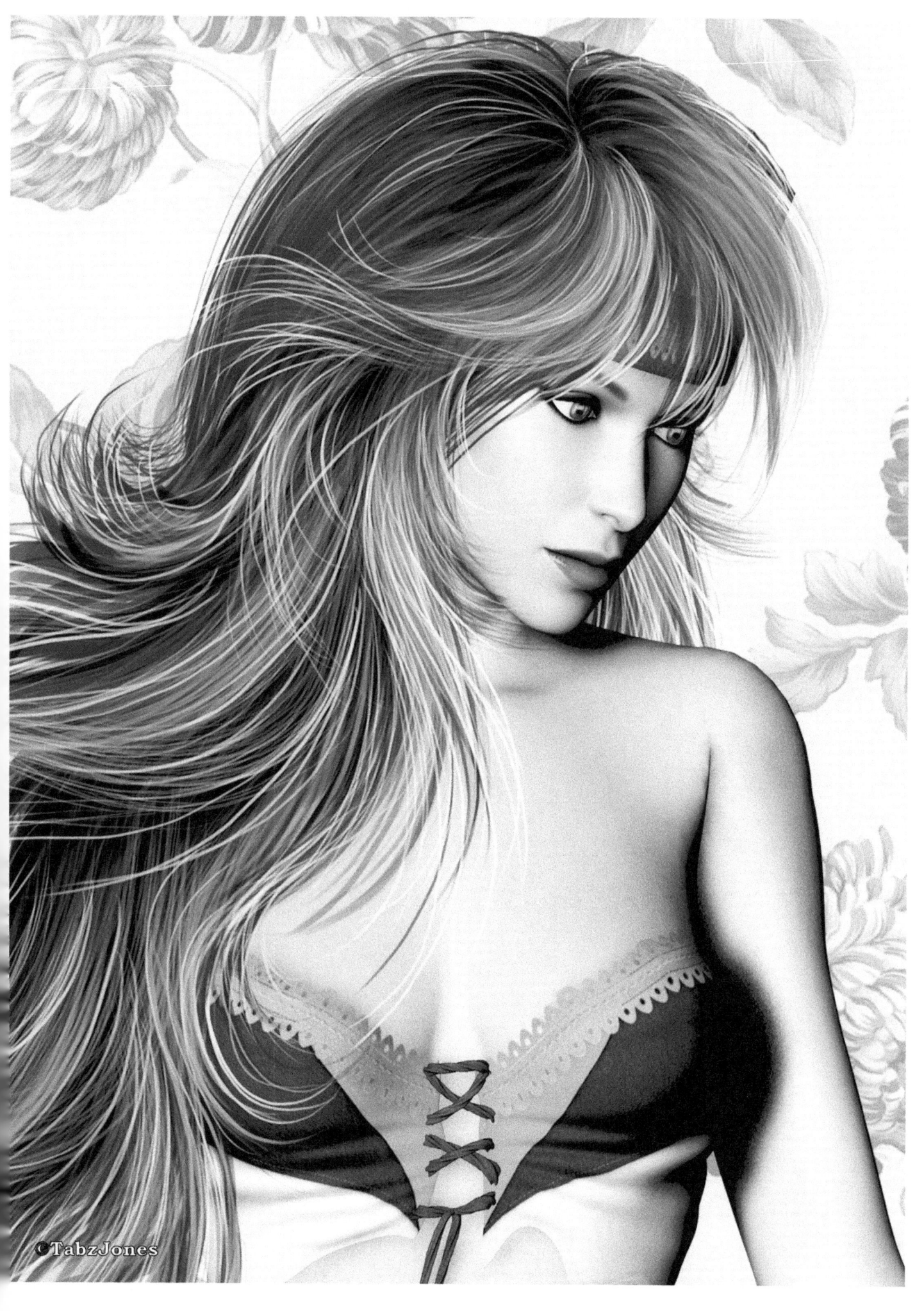

©TabzJones

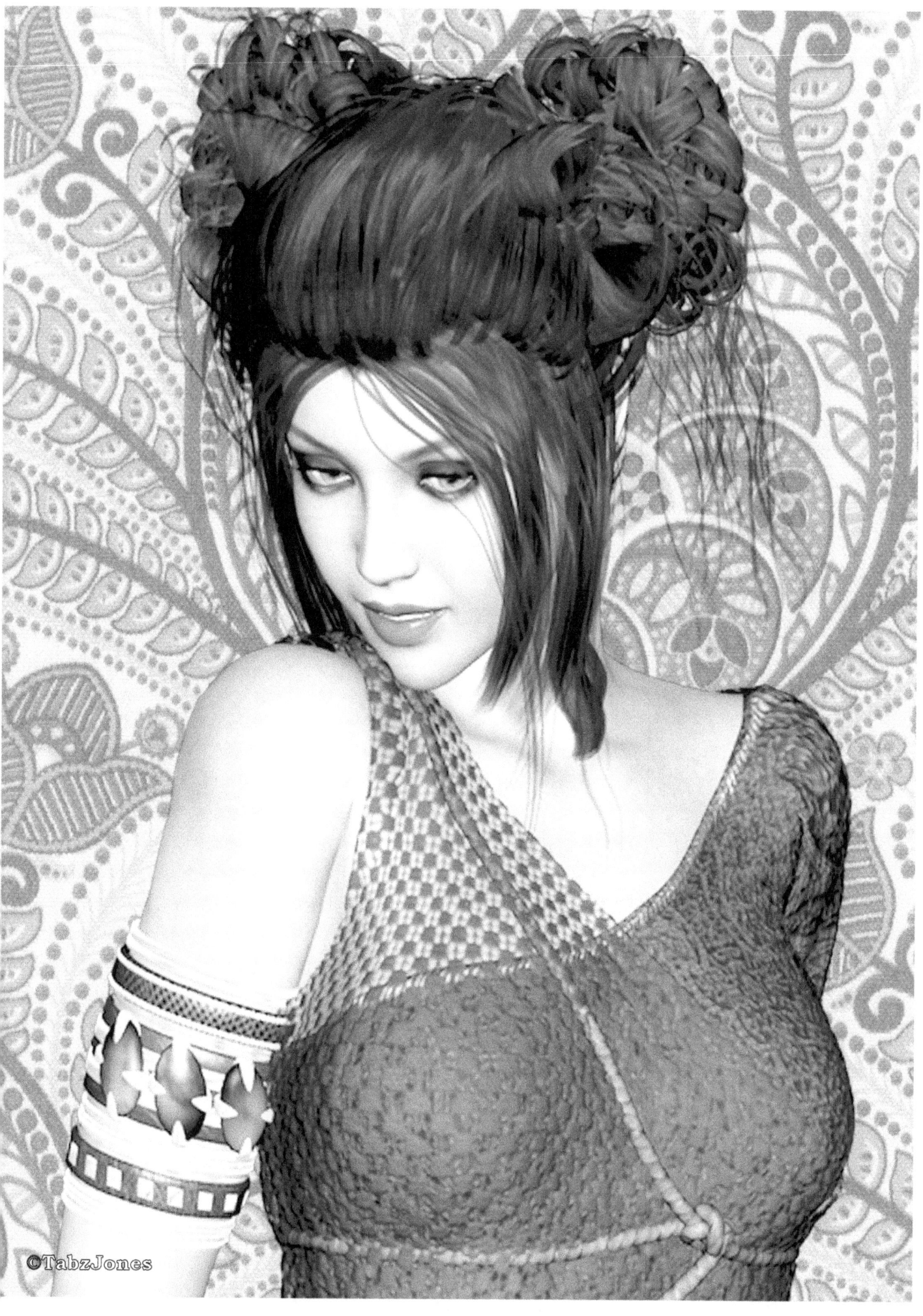

©TabzJones

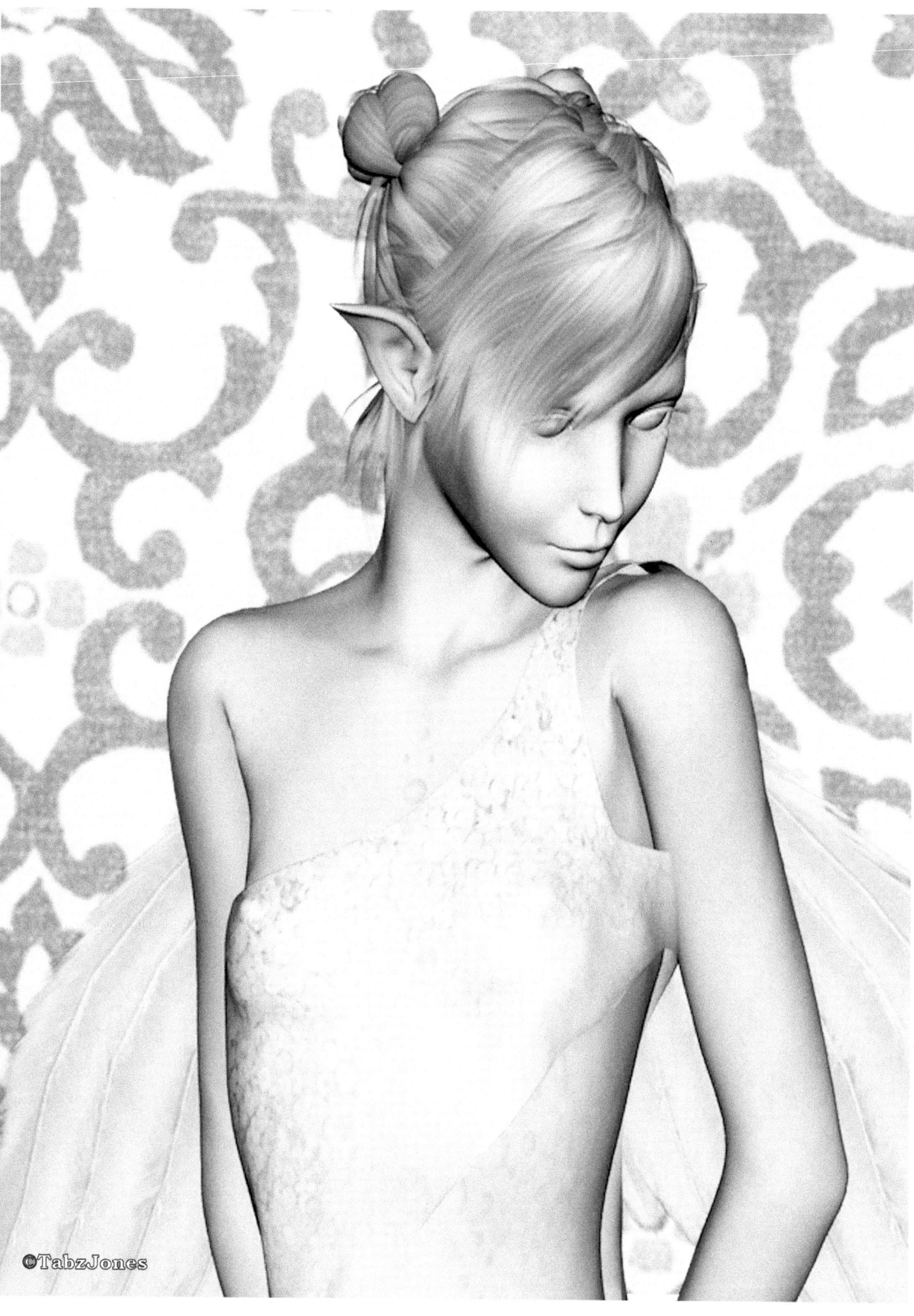

©TabzJones

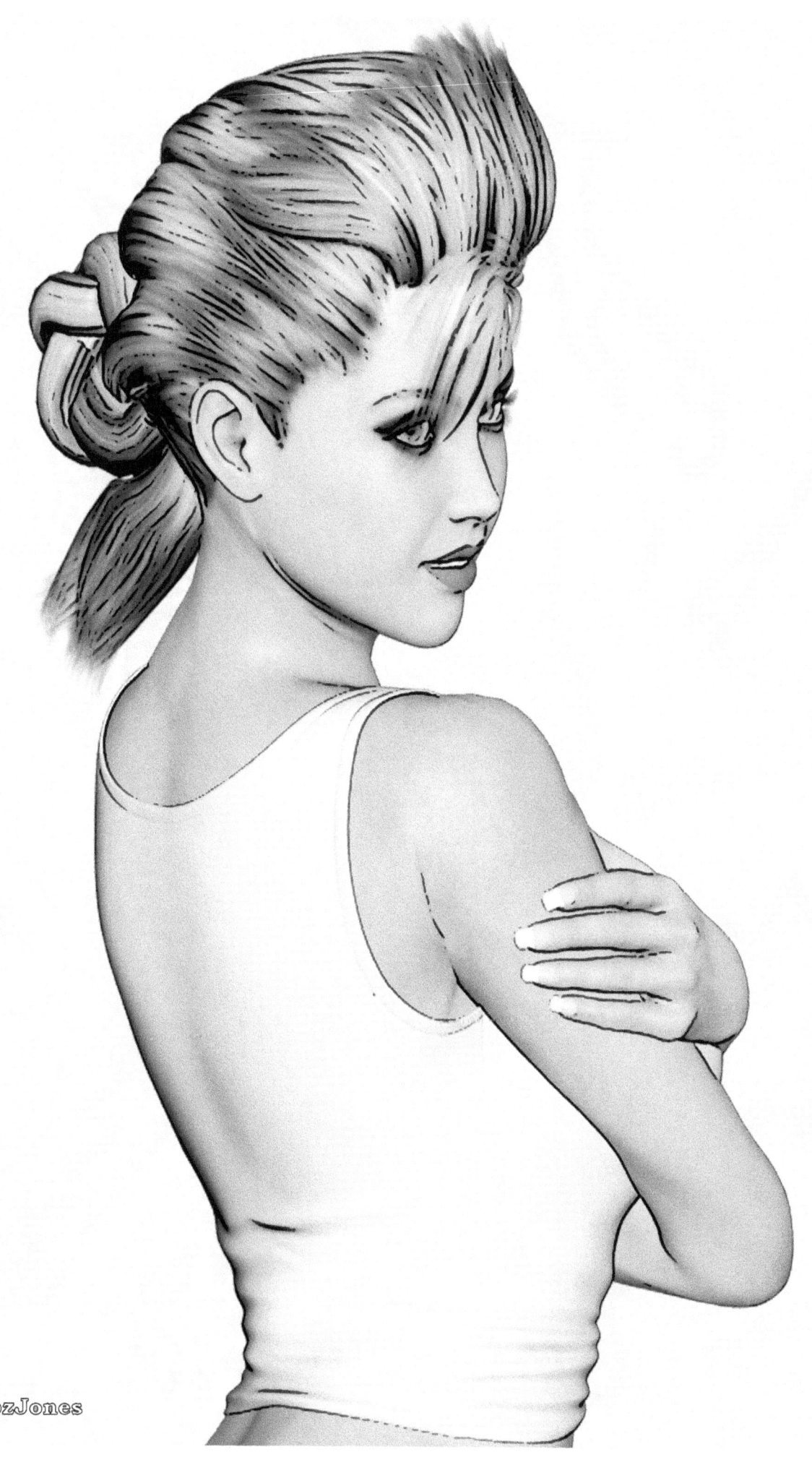

©TabzJones

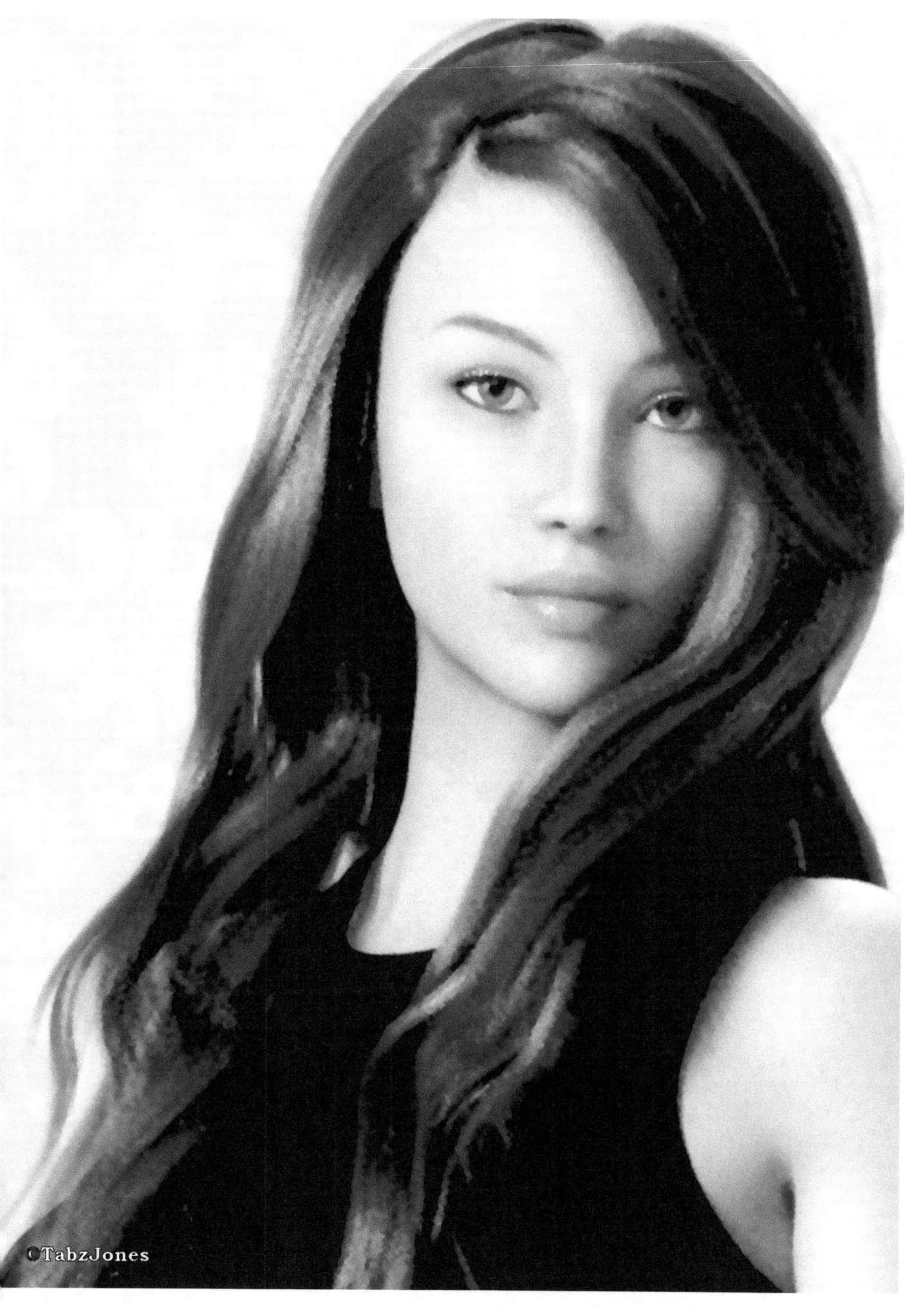

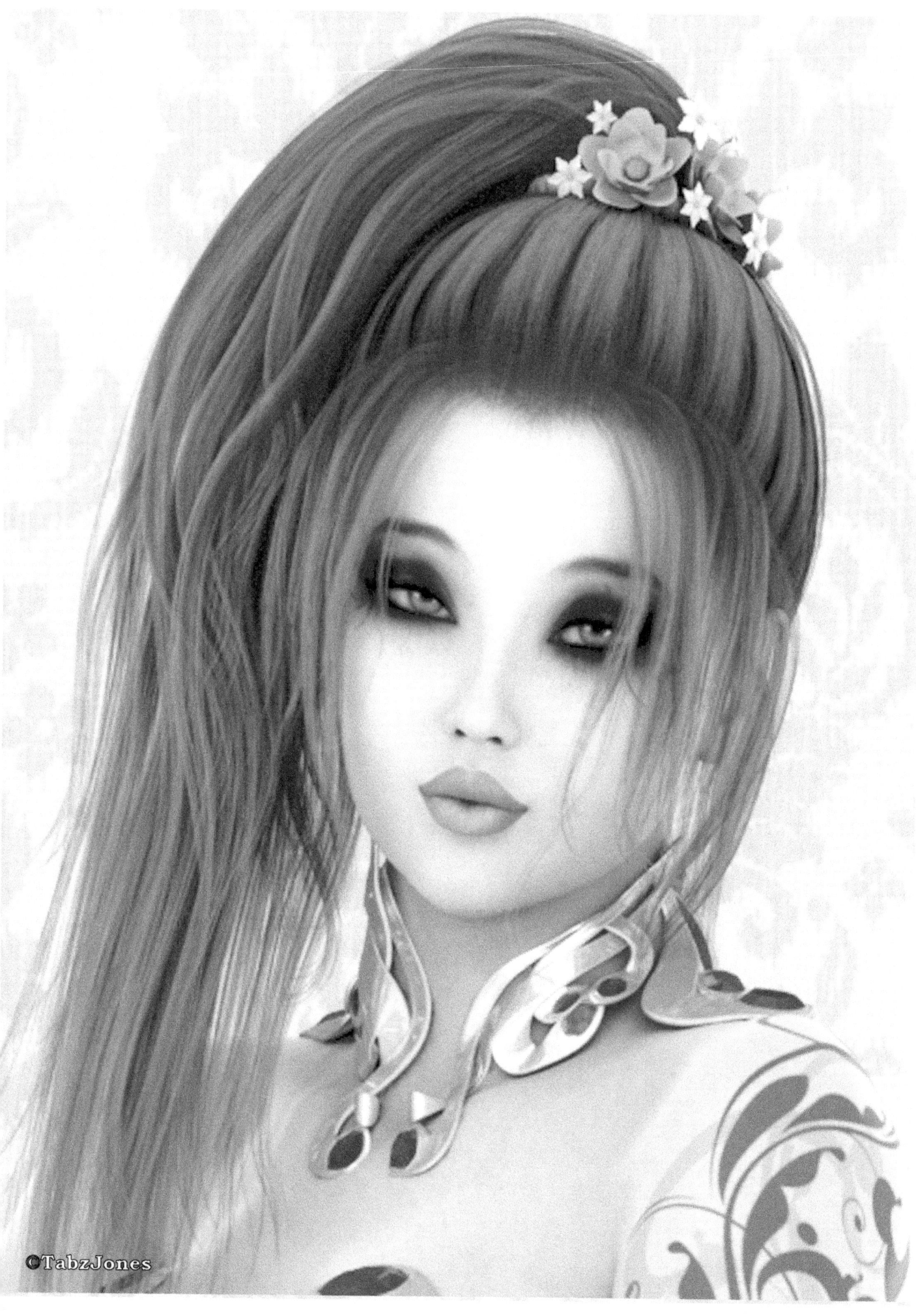
©TabzJones

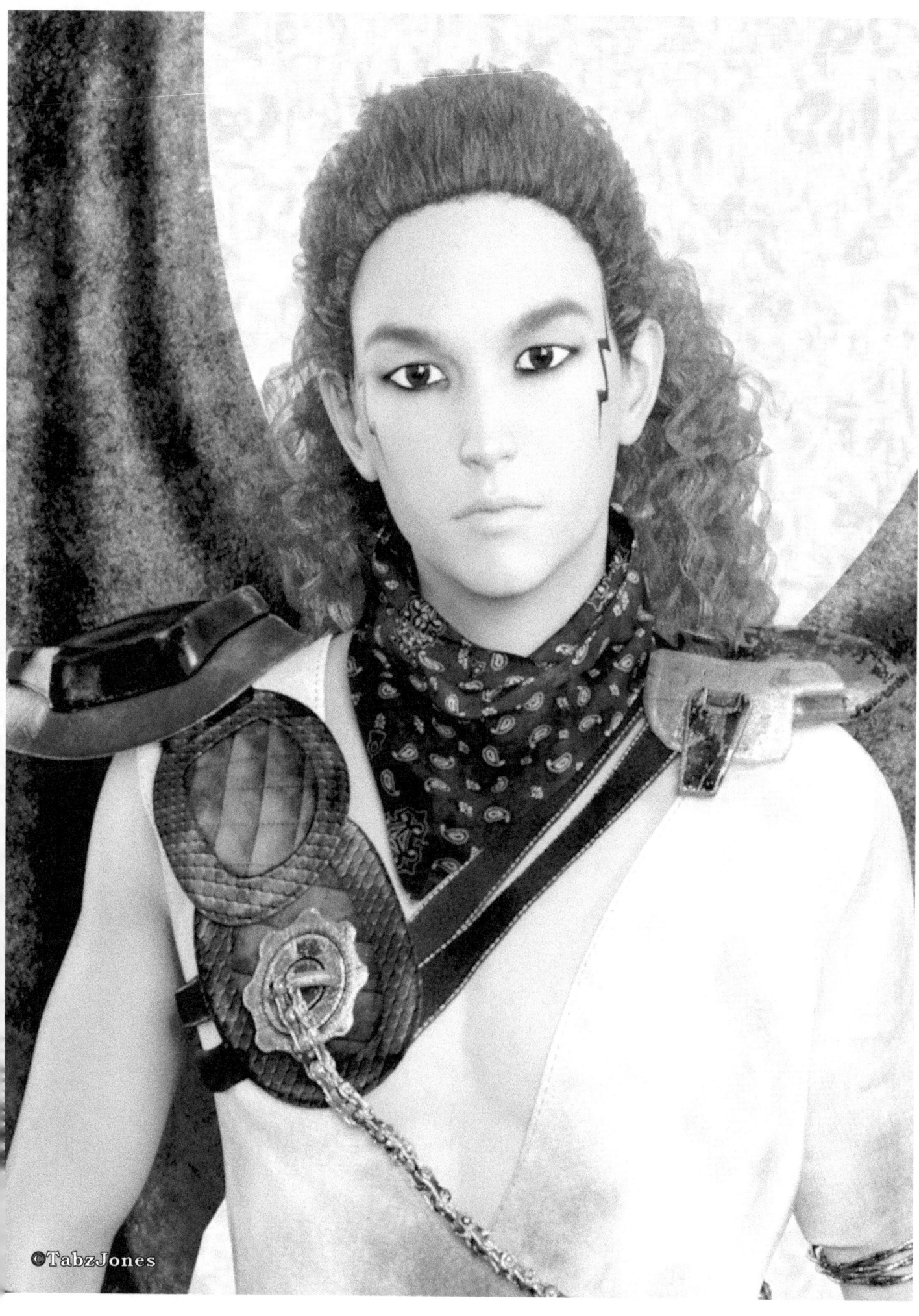

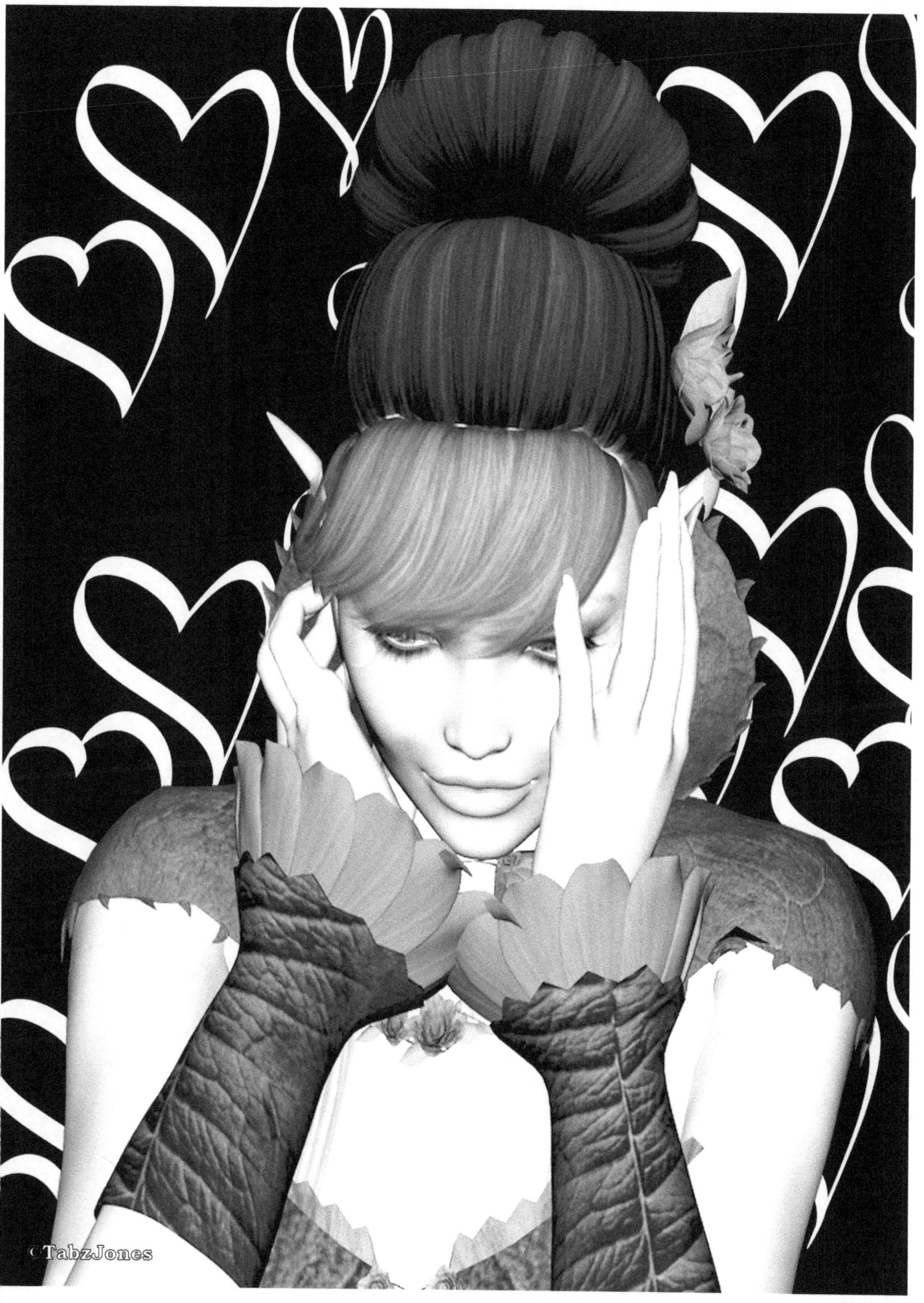

©TabzJones

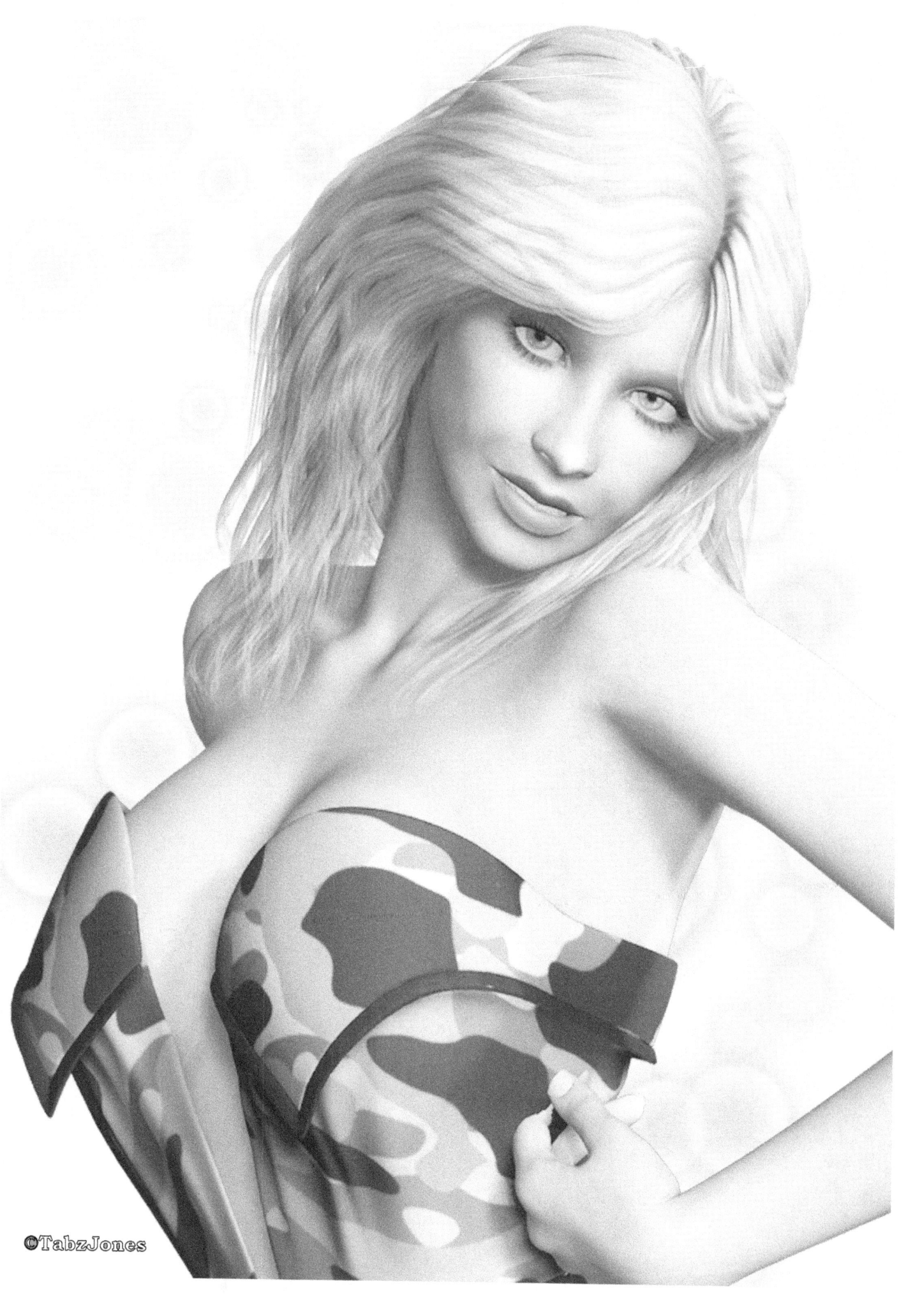
©TabzJones

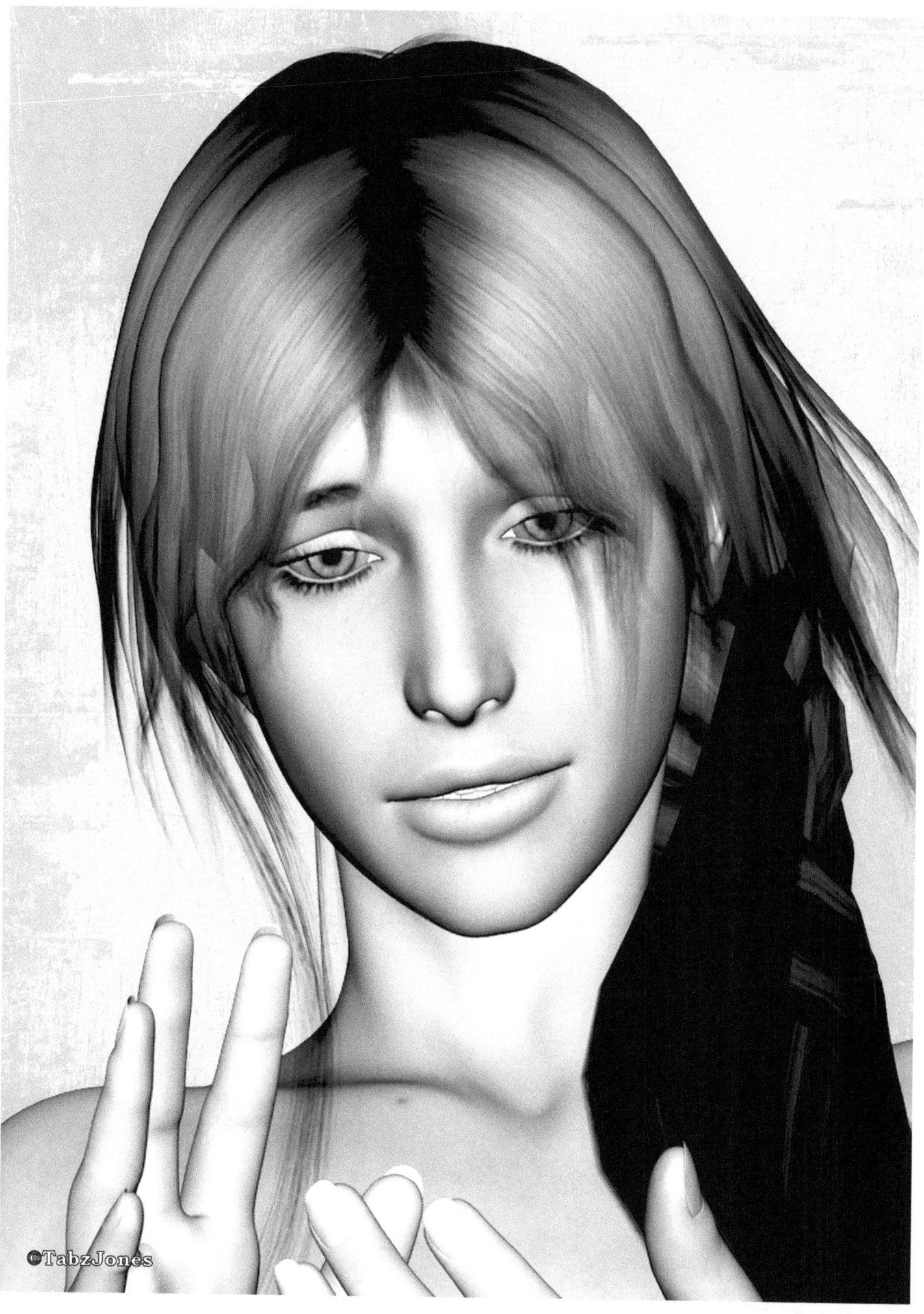

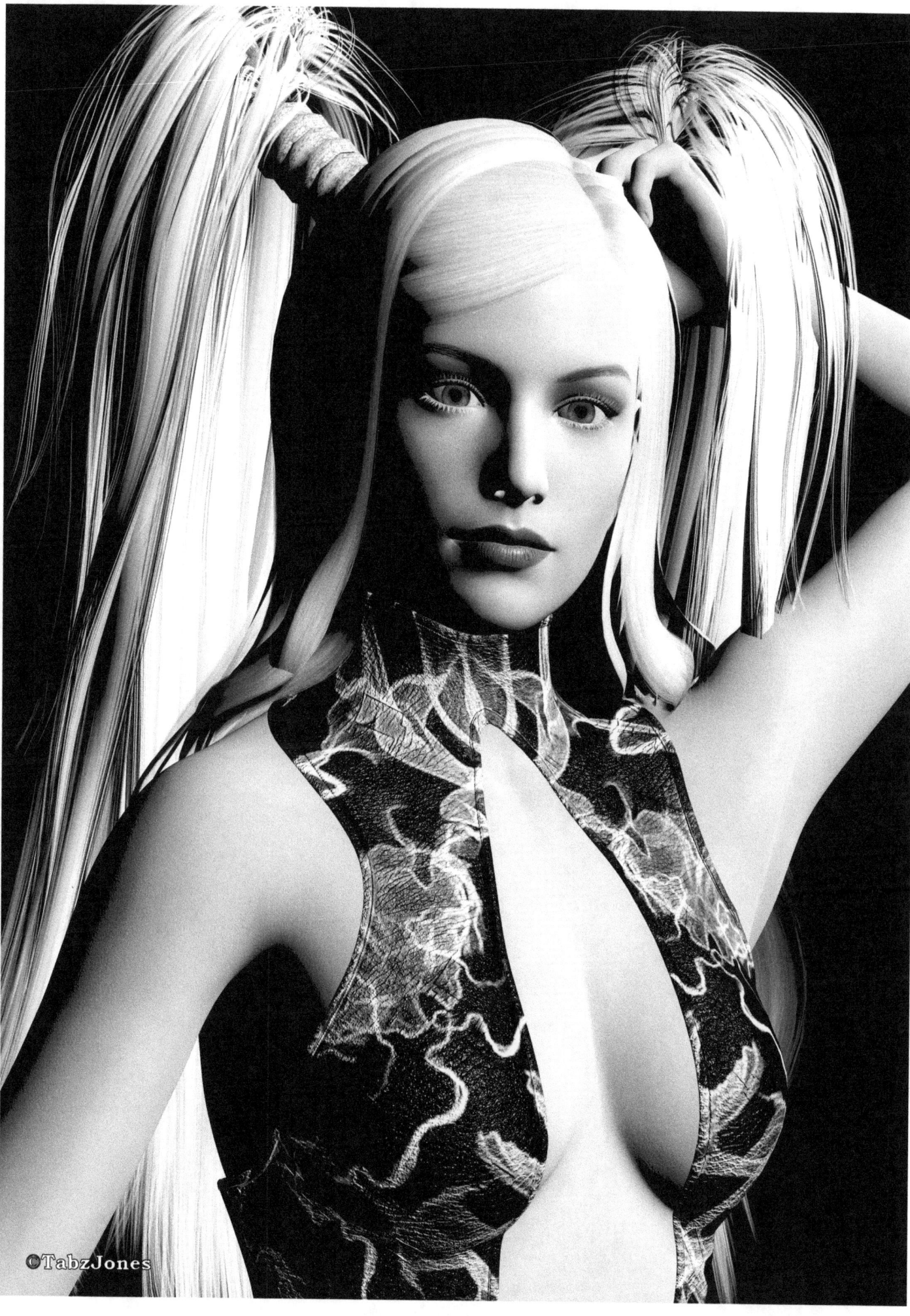

©TabzJones

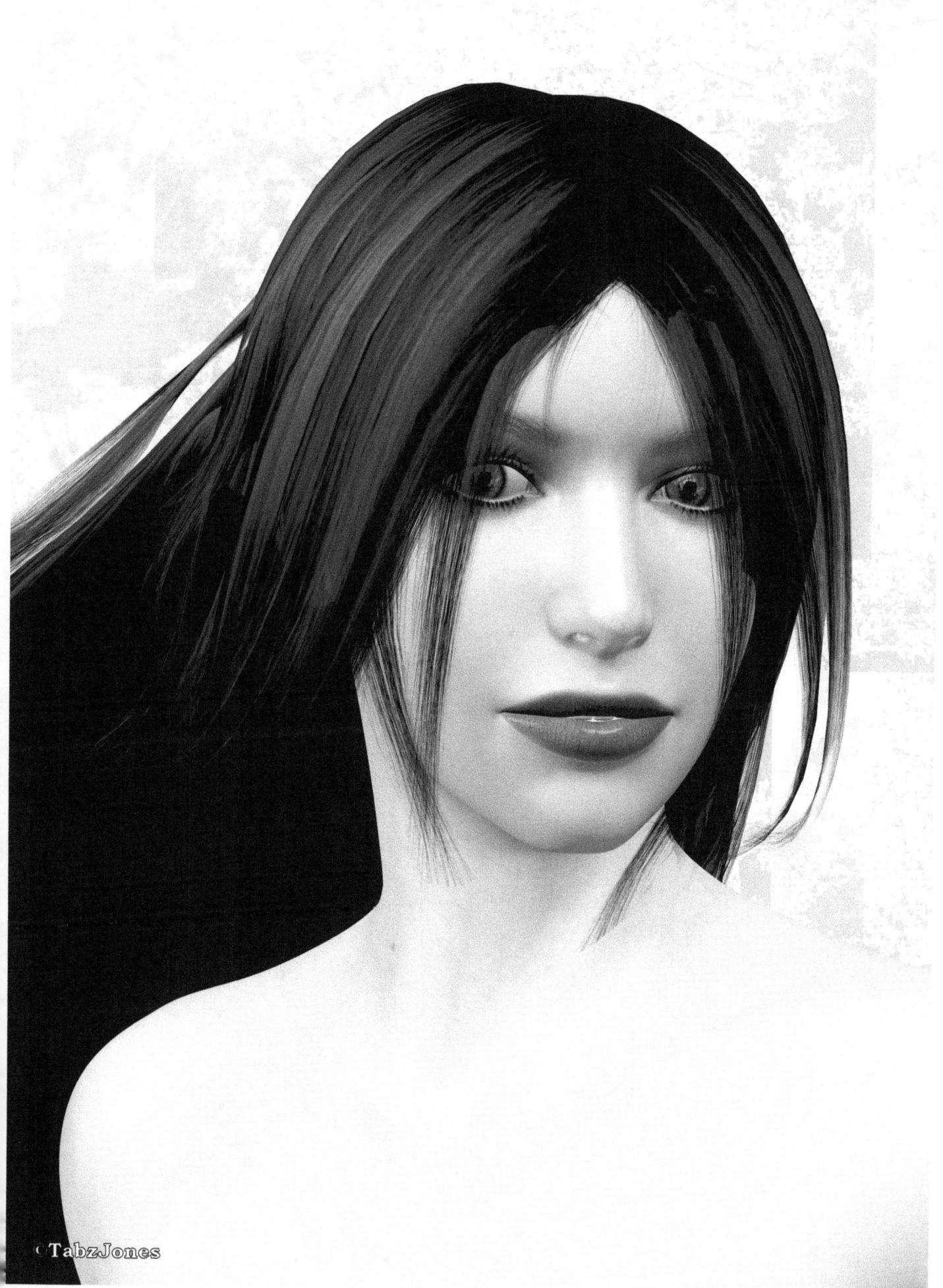

©TabzJones

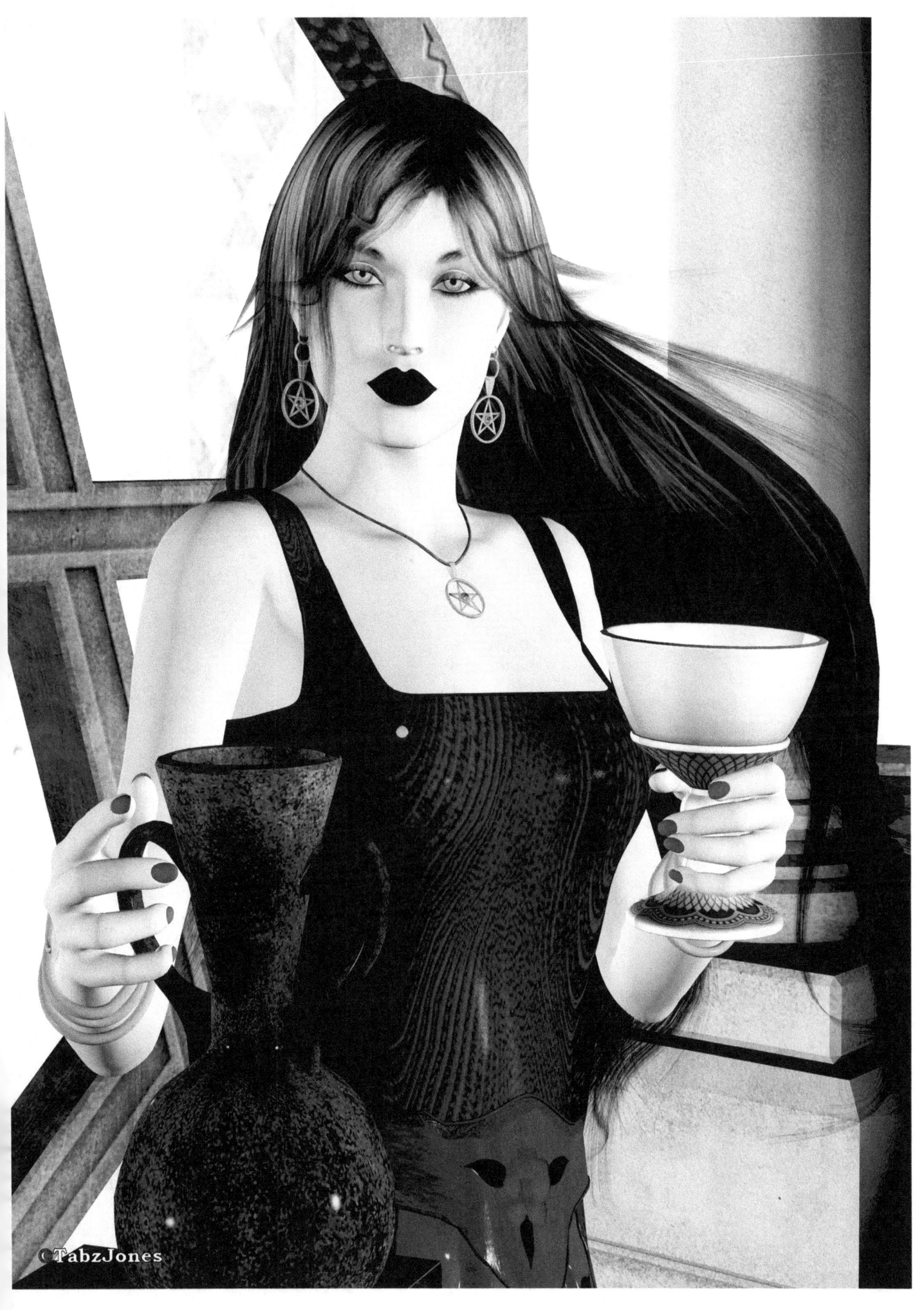

©TabzJones

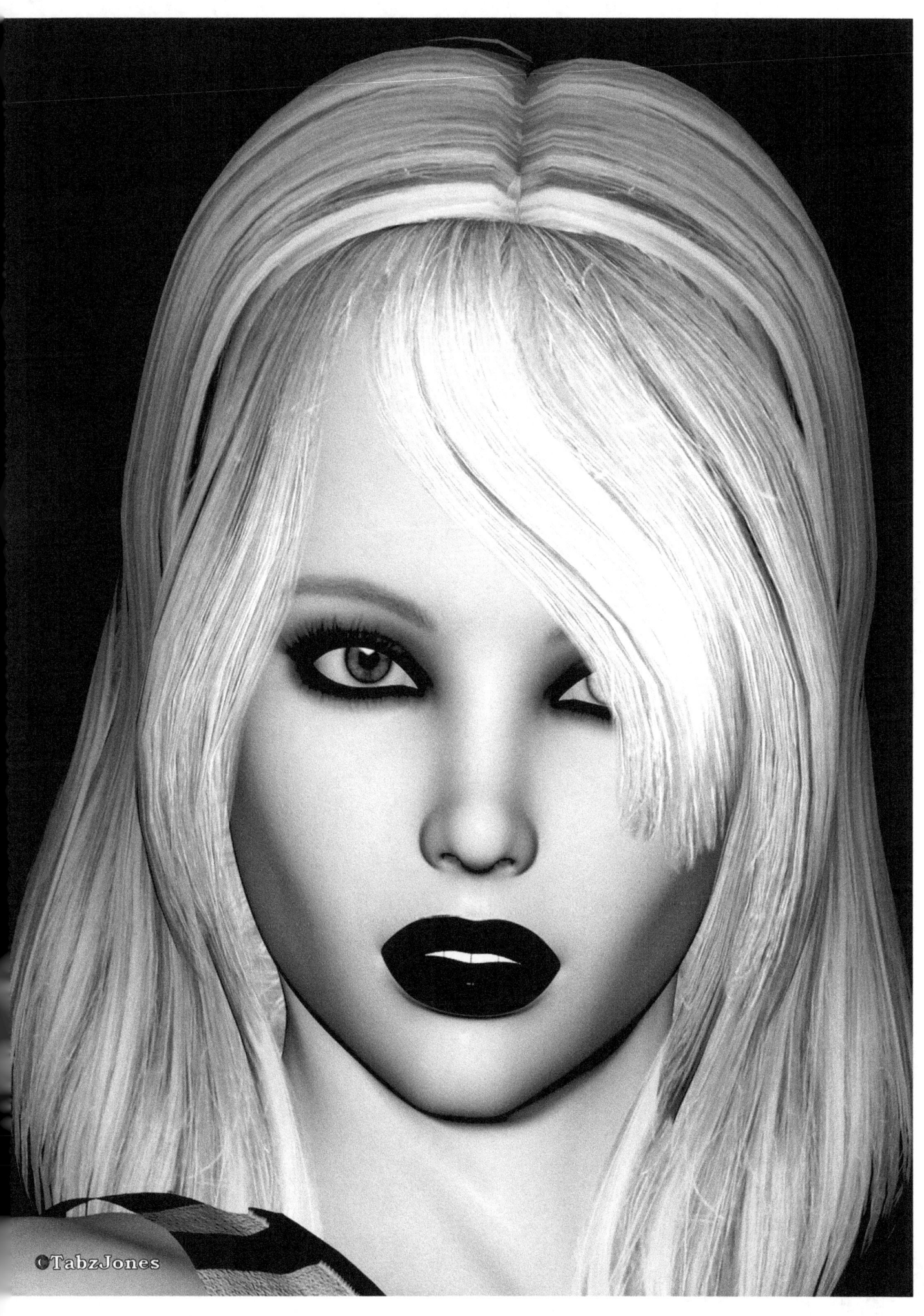

©TabzJones

www.ingramcontent.com/pod-product-compliance
Lightning Source LLC
Chambersburg PA
CBHW080602190526

45169CB00007B/2848